WORK

BEVERLEY SHEPHERD

Other titles in the *Life Issues* series:

Forgiveness, Ron Kallmier ISBN 978-1-85345-446-2
Relationships, Lynn Penson ISBN 978-1-85345-447-9
Environment, Ruth Valerio ISBN 978-1-85345-481-3

For further details of CWR's ministry visit: www.cwr.org.uk

CONTENTS

INTRODUCTION

For many of us, over half our waking hours are spent working – whether in paid employment, studying, caring for children or the general maintenance functions of cooking, cleaning and grocery shopping. It is surprising, therefore, that over the last few decades the Church has had little to say on the subject, with few people having heard a sermon about work and a lack of applications of general biblical teaching being made to the workplace. As a result, the impression has been given that God is not interested in our work, or that the only areas of work that God values are those concerned with mission, the 'caring' professions and charity or aid agencies. The role of paid employment in the Christian life has been relegated to the source of money for supplying our daily needs or funding Christian mission/church. Somehow what happens when Christians are gathered in the church building is deemed to be more important than how they behave when they leave to take up their roles in family, society and the workplace. How did this happen?

The seeds of this sacred/secular divide were planted at the beginning of the fifth century by Augustine, a significant figure in Church history. He was deeply influenced by Greek thought which believed that the spirit or non-material world was vastly superior to the material world. The key to life was contemplation and so anything to do with work was negative. Leisure was what you aimed for and so the Roman word for business in Latin was *neg-otium* or 'not leisure'. The Greek way of thinking, which infiltrated the Church, is totally counter to the Hebrew worldview which sees all of life as important to God. Thumb through Leviticus and you will see that God is concerned with fraud, the timely payment of wages, the variety of seeds you plant in the one field, dishonest weights and measures and the selling of property.

If we reclaim our Hebrew heritage and see our work as important to God it can re-energise us. Knowing that He has a purpose for those hours of our week can lead us to seek His wisdom, power and enabling for all that it entails. It is in the workplace that we also find our greatest opportunity to transform our nation! As Mark Greene says:

> ... I am convinced that Britain will never be transformed until the laity use the opportunities for influence daily afforded by their various professions,

crafts and occupations. In other words, if we want better laws, it is politicians and lawyers who make them. If we want better education, it is teachers and educationalists who will mould it. If we want more ethical medicine, it is doctors, nurses and technicians who will shape that for us. If we want more honest business, it must come from more honest businesspeople. If we want to see a change in our culture, it will happen usually on the inside.[1]

Using the Material:

This set of studies is designed to be used in a group setting, though an individual can use it by adapting the group work as appropriate. Each group will handle the material differently but here are a few suggestions to help you get the most out of it.

- This study guide is about work. In the first study we explore various definitions of work. It is important to be inclusive and not just limit discussions to paid employment. Encourage those that work in the home, those who are job-seeking and those who are 'retired' to share about their work.
- These studies will work more effectively if each person is encouraged to read through the material before coming together to discuss it.
- It might be helpful for each person to use a notebook to jot down answers, thoughts and reflections both during the sessions and between times together, although there is space to write in this book.
- At the end of each study there are some suggestions for prayer. Do not feel limited by these – they are designed to pick up the themes of the study and to acknowledge our need of the Holy Spirit and each other.
- It would be helpful for the leader/facilitator to be familiar with the questions and activities in order to adapt them to the specific needs of the group.
- It is important that people feel they can be honest without being judged and that they are assured of confidentiality.
- Enjoy and have some fun!

SITUATION VACANT

◎ Chill out

Each member of the group is given a piece of paper on which you each write the answer to the question: 'What did you want to be when you grew up?' One person gathers all the papers, numbers them, and the group members each decide who was No. 1, then No. 2 etc. A prize for the most correctly identified answers will be at the discretion of the group leader!

◎ Think through

Imagine your current job (whether in paid employment, working in the home, job-searching or retired) advertised in the 'Situations vacant' column of the newspaper. Your job description, salary, working environment and reporting structure are all detailed.

- What aspects of the job would cause you to apply, and what parts would put you off applying?
- Share with the group your thoughts about the positives and negatives of your job.

INVESTIGATE:

- What is work?
- Does God work?
- Is work a curse resulting from the Fall, or was it part of God's perfect creation?

WORK

Various words throughout the Bible are translated 'work' and they each have a different emphasis: 'an act', 'a doing', 'energy', 'labour', 'weariness', 'toil', 'trade'. Work is certainly not limited to paid employment.

Some definitions may prove helpful:

- Work: 'effort directed to an end.' *Chambers Twentieth Century Dictionary*
- Work that pleases God: 'the expenditure of energy (manual or mental or both) in the service of others, which brings fulfilment to the worker, benefit to the community, and glory to God.' John Stott[1]
- Work: 'purposeful and indispensable activity to meet human needs and aspirations.' *Dictionary of Pastoral Care*[2]
- 'Human work is sharing in God's work: it is the expenditure of human energy in the mastery of the world and the development of human life, using the resources of God's creation.' Bishop Graham Dow[3]

Genesis starts with the account of God's creative activity. He spoke into being every aspect of our world – light, darkness, sky, waters, dry ground, vegetation, fruit, sun, moon, stars, day, night, birds, fish, animals and, finally, mankind. As Psalm 8:3 records: 'When I consider your heavens, the *work of your fingers*, the moon and the stars, which you have set in place ...' (my emphasis). At the end of each carefully planned phase of His creation God celebrated what He had made: 'It is good.' A sense of pleasure in His work is conveyed. In the New Testament we see Jesus, God incarnate, working as a carpenter.

So God is presented in Genesis 1 as 'God the Worker'; and human beings are like this because they are in the image of God. God is the archetypal worker, the one in whom all human work finds its meaning. Human work, therefore, cannot be understood apart from God's work in creation. Our work is meant to be a reflection of his creativity. The work we are to do in our daily occupation is God's work; we are partners with him in it.[4]

We are made in the image of a God who works. It should not surprise us therefore that God gave us the gift of work before the Fall. In Genesis 2:15 we read: 'The Lord God took the man and put him in the Garden of Eden to work it and take care of it.' Work is God-ordained and was, from the beginning, part of God's purpose for men and women. The fact that it remains part of God's purpose for us is evidenced by the fourth commandment: 'Remember the Sabbath day by keeping it holy. Six days you shall labour and do all your work ...' (Exod. 20:8).

WHY WORK?

INVESTIGATE:
Read Ecclesiastes 5:18–20.
- Think of all the benefits of having work to do – and list them.
- Why do you do your current job?

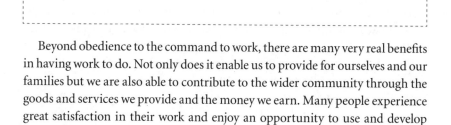

Beyond obedience to the command to work, there are many very real benefits in having work to do. Not only does it enable us to provide for ourselves and our families but we are also able to contribute to the wider community through the goods and services we provide and the money we earn. Many people experience great satisfaction in their work and enjoy an opportunity to use and develop their skills. Some individuals value the sociability of their working environment and the opportunity to meet a range of different people. And others enjoy the challenge of their role and the sense of achievement it brings.

In visiting the 'Work' exhibit at the Millennium Dome I was struck that only one of the three rooms depicted the positive aspects and creativity of work – the other two conveyed more of the futility, drudgery and pressure of work that some experience. The first room was filled floor to ceiling with cage upon cage – each containing a rodent on a treadmill. The second was similarly covered floor to ceiling – this time with yellow Post-it® notes on each of which was written one more thing for the 'to do' list.

For many people work demands increasing amounts of time and energy, leaving them emotionally or physically exhausted. The pressure to meet targets or deadlines can lead to constant anxiety; whilst the need, in some organisations, to make cutbacks can cause fear of redundancy.

WORK AND THE FALL

INVESTIGATE:
Read: Genesis 3:17–19.
- What was the effect of God's curse on Adam's work?
- What effects of this curse do you see on your own work?

The entrance of sin into the world and the resulting curse changed work from a joy into weary toil. The context for our work is now cursed so the photocopier will break down on occasion, the computer system will crash when we most need to access an important document, our train may well be late, our colleagues will sometimes fail to deliver to a deadline and customers will not always be right. Projects in which we have invested hours of work will get cancelled and meaningless changes will be made to systems that operate effectively as they are. With the writer of Ecclesiastes we will be tempted to declare:

So I hated life, because the work that is done under the sun was grievous to me. All of it is meaningless, a chasing after the wind. I hated all the things I had toiled for under the sun, because I must leave them to the one who comes after me. And who knows whether he will be a wise man or a fool? Yet he will have control over all the work into which I have poured my effort and skill under the sun. This too is meaningless. So my heart began to despair over all my toilsome labour under the sun.

Ecclesiastes 2:17–20

The Boss

The person for whom we work can have a significant effect on how we experience our working day. Our 'bosses' can set the tone for the whole working environment, give helpful feedback to help us develop or devastating criticism through which we feel belittled. They can explain the value of the work and convey a sense of purpose or fail to communicate either.

Your boss is not an unfortunate obstacle in your path to spiritual maturity, but far more likely to be an instrument in God's hand to bring about that spiritual maturity. God is in control of our bosses. And he is in control even when they have lost control, when circumstances arise in which they are unable to act on our behalf even though they might want to.[5]

INVESTIGATE:
- What is your attitude to your boss/manager/supervisor?
- How do you see your responsibilities to those who report to you?

Read Colossians 3:22–4:1.
- What difference does the knowledge that we are 'working [as] for the Lord' (that He is the One to whom we ultimately report) make to the way we do our work?
- What difference does it make to our relationships with those to whom we report and those who report to us?

There is a story told of the great preacher, Charles Spurgeon. Speaking to a young woman who was a member of his congregation and who worked as a domestic servant, he asked: 'What difference does being a Christian make to the way you do your work?' She replied 'I now sweep under the mats!'

We are called to: 'Serve wholeheartedly, as if you were serving the Lord, not men ...' (Eph. 6:7). It can be difficult to 'go the second mile' when you feel time pressured and resentful of the demands already placed on you. In conducting the training of a series of team-building courses for a large IT company, I was asked to spend the first evening having dinner with the delegates. As I had a few of these courses each month it meant giving up several precious evenings. I had my excuses at the ready: 'the delegates need a break from me' (and vice versa!); 'they would feel greater freedom to relax if I were not around' etc. Then I read Luke 15 when Jesus was criticised by the Pharisees for welcoming and eating with sinners. He goes on to demonstrate through the three 'lost' parables that God's agenda is firmly set on seeking and saving the lost. It was as if God were saying, 'Bev, you work for Me remember, and *I* want you to have dinner with the delegates!' These dinners proved to be privileged times.

Pray for each other

Take time in your group to pray for each other:

- For those seeking work
- For the aspects of your work that you find difficult
- For your managers and supervisors
- For yourselves – that you would be more conscious of God's presence at work
  And finally,
- Praise God for all the benefits work brings

THE JOB DESCRIPTION

◎ Chill out

Think of one person at work to whom you would like to be a blessing in the coming week. Share with the group who they are and why you chose them.

◎ Think through

Those of us in paid employment are used to having a detailed job description outlining all the key aspects of our role, areas of accountability, our working hours, the reporting structure and the ubiquitous 'anything else that may be expected'. Those working in the home may well envy this seeming clarity! What, though, is the job description for a Christian in the workplace? Many of us muddle through without any clear idea of what God may expect of us at work, or fearful of asking in case it involves career-damaging evangelism by the coffee machine! Is it enough just 'to do a good job'? Should I make a point of mentioning that I go to church? What if I don't live up to my colleagues' expectations of how a Christian should act? Or, as one research manager put it: 'Please don't ask me to think about being a Christian at work – my job is hard enough as it is!'

INVESTIGATE:

- What do you think the job description of a 'Christian at work' is?

Read Genesis 12:1–3.

- We know from Galatians 3:6–9 that we are inheritors of the Abrahamic covenant. What might this mean in your workplace?

God calls Abram and makes a covenant with him – God will bless him and he in turn will be a blessing. We are inheritors of that promise! We are called to both be blessed and to be channels of God's blessing wherever we go – including our places of work. You and I are God's pipeline of blessing into this fallen world. How then are we to fulfil so great a calling?

In the context of the workplace there are four ways we can do this: by being a MODEL, a MINISTER, a MOVER & SHAKER and a MOUTHPIECE. Being a model is foundational for all Christians; the other roles are linked to opportunity and gifting.

MODEL

Every time you walk into your place of work, you are on a catwalk. Your audience of managers, colleagues and customers is critically appraising your 'outfit' and assessing: 'Does it fit?' 'Is it worth what it cost you?' 'Would it suit me?' Their answers to such questions may depend on whether you are modelling a straitjacket of 'Thou shalt knots' or a designer coat of many colours!

You are called to create envy! God's intention in calling a people to Himself in Exodus is that other nations should look at how blessed Israel was through living in relationship with the Lord Almighty and want it for themselves! Joseph's 'richly ornamented robe' was a sign of his father's great love for him, and the other brothers knew it and were envious (Gen. 37:3–4). First and foremost we model being God's beloved sons and daughters. We walk through those office, factory, hospital or school doors knowing that we are accepted and loved by our Heavenly Father, and that there is not one thing that is going to happen today that is going to change that.

A couple of years ago I was training delegates on a leadership course for one of the American airlines. My co-trainer spent much of our free time asking about my faith in God. At one point she exclaimed: 'You make it sound so good!' She envied a relationship that you and I know to be the right of all who receive Jesus – the right to become children of God (John 1:12).

INVESTIGATE:
Read Daniel 6:1–14.
- In what ways did Daniel 'model' his relationship with God?
- What impact did this have on the king and on the administrators/satraps?
- In what ways are you able to 'model' to others your relationship with your Heavenly Father?

MINISTER

For many of our colleagues life is not easy. Behind the smiling masks there are relationship breakdowns, addictions, bereavement, debt, worry and fear. Work is rarely a safe place to let anyone see behind the mask, especially if that painful situation is relayed, with embellishments, down the office grapevine. Yet the workplace is our place of ministry – where we are brought into contact with a hurting, sinful world and asked to bind its wounds and wash its feet. But it takes time to love my neighbour and the workplace is task-focused and hectic. Giving people time and a confidential ear can be costly.

Every day I put love on the line. There is nothing I am less good at than love. I am far better in competition than love. I am far better at responding to my instincts and ambitions to get ahead and make my mark than I am at figuring out how to love another. I am schooled and trained in acquisitive skills, in getting my own way. And yet, I decide every day to set aside what I can do best and attempt what I do very clumsily – open myself up to the frustrations and failures of loving, daring to believe that failing in love is better than succeeding in pride.[1]

I was struck by the power of love in action when a speaker, Anne*, shared a personal example. Anne worked in advertising – a business characterised by great competitiveness. Her colleague, Jennifer*, was disliked for being arrogant, abrasive and using questionable tactics to land new clients. En route to work Anne remembered that Jennifer was to hold an important meeting with a very prestigious prospective client that day. Her initial thoughts weren't so honourable: 'I kind of hoped she wouldn't get the contract. She was so difficult to work with! And, I admit, I felt very competitive too.' Then suddenly, words from 1 Corinthians popped into her head: Love 'looks for a way of being constructive … has good manners and does not pursue selfish advantage' (Phillips). Anne felt challenged: 'Maybe I should wish Jennifer well. Even go out of my way to encourage her! She did seem a little nervous …'

Anne passed a stall with gorgeous bouquets of spring flowers. 'Flowers? No, my colleagues will think I'm strange if I do this for Jennifer! Hardly anyone really wants her to succeed.' BUT – convinced God had brought Jennifer to mind and believing her role in the workplace was to be constructive and to love others, Anne chose a large colourful bouquet. On the card she simply wrote: 'I wish you well today in your important meeting' and signed her name.

Jennifer was not yet in when Anne placed the bouquet on her desk. A colleague saw her coming out of Jennifer's office and teased her, but deep down Anne felt good about her action. Later Jennifer walked into Anne's office, with tears in her eyes. 'Thank you for the flowers – I had no idea anyone cared about how I did today.'[2] (*Names have been changed.)

One of the primary ways we minister to those around us is through the work we do. I am blessed by those who return my phone calls, complete work when they say they will and on whom you can rely to do a good job.

INVESTIGATE:
Read 2 Kings 5:1–3.
- What might have been the servant girl's attitude to working in Naaman's household?
- How did she minister to 'her boss'?
- Share examples of where you have been in a position to bring care/comfort/counsel/prayer to those with whom you work.

MOVER & SHAKER

Movers & Shakers are called to change the world! (Or, at least, that part of it they occupy – be it systems, codes of practice, laws or attitudes.) The work is long-term and can be discouraging. It is a role that needs the support and prayer of other Christians. William Wilberforce is a prime example:

> *... William Wilberforce came within a hair's breadth of missing his grand calling altogether. His faith in Jesus Christ animated his lifelong passion for reform ... But when Wilberforce came to faith ... at the age of twenty-five, his first reaction was to throw over politics for the ministry. He thought, as millions have thought before and since, that 'spiritual' affairs are far more important than 'secular' affairs. Fortunately, a minister, John Newton, persuaded Wilberforce that God wanted him to stay in politics rather than enter the ministry. 'It's hoped and believed,' Newton wrote, 'that the Lord has raised you up for the good of the nation.'* [3]

INVESTIGATE:
Read Isaiah 58.
* Are there any work situations where God is calling you to 'loose the chains of injustice' or 'do away with the yoke of oppression'?

MOUTHPIECE

'They overcame him [the devil] by the blood of the Lamb and by the word of their testimony; they did not love their lives so much as to shrink from death' (Rev. 12:11).

The word of our testimony is important. We are fortunate in this country that declaring our faith is unlikely to lead to physical death – yet it may mean the death of our career prospects, our image or even some of our friendships. It is natural to shrink from potential loss and so stay silent. Esther is a helpful role model to us. When she explains to her uncle, Mordecai, that if she approaches the king without his permission she may be killed, his reply is:

'Do not think that because you are in the king's house you alone of all the Jews will escape. For if you remain silent at this time, relief and deliverance for the Jews will arise from another place, but you and your father's family will perish. And who knows but that you have come to royal position for such a time as this?' (Esth. 4:13–14).

INVESTIGATE:
Read Esther 4:15–5:8.
- How did Esther prepare for her audience with the king?
- What fears may she have experienced?
- Why do you think she did not present her request initially (Esth. 5:3)?
- How important is our relationship with a person when seeking to witness?
- What inhibits us in speaking to others about our faith?

Esther's reaction to this situation is instructive:
- She prays and asks others to pray
- She dresses in her royal robes – a coat of many colours?
- Despite the king's extravagant promise, she does not take advantage of the situation by mentioning the edict (which was irrevocable). This would have embarrassed him in front of the whole court.
- She restores relationship by inviting him to dinner, twice.
- She awaits the right time before making her request.
- She does not allow fear of death to prevent her from speaking.

SUMMARY:
- Which role do you most identify with – that of Minister, Mover & Shaker or Mouthpiece?
- What would help you to develop – either further in that role or in one of the other roles?

Pray for each other
Spend time praying for each other, picking up on some of the discussion about being a Model, a Minister, a Mover & Shaker and a Mouthpiece.

LEARNING AND DEVELOPMENT

◎ Chill out

At the beginning of the last study members of the group spoke about who, in their workplace, they wanted to bless in the coming week. Invite people to share what happened.

◎ Think through

Throughout our working life there are opportunities to grow, develop our skills, gain experience and face new challenges. Sometimes this occurs through being coached by someone more experienced, going on training courses, personal study or simply through watching others.

Jesus was a trainer – He taught His disciples, He modelled good practice, He set them practical exercises and He debriefed them afterwards. And He didn't expect them to get everything right! God is in the business of growing and developing us as His disciples. The workplace is an ideal environment for this to happen because of the pressures we experience there, the people we have to work with and the sheer amount of time we spend at work.

What is God training us for? I believe He is training us:

- To do our current jobs well
- To prepare us for promotion
- To develop our character.

We will look at each in turn.

TO DO OUR CURRENT JOBS WELL

For each of us to do our job well – whether we are the Chief Executive of a multi-million-pound business, stacking shelves in the local supermarket, home schooling our children or filling prescriptions at the local chemist – we need both skill and wisdom.

To become skilled takes hard work. Jesus would have been trained by his father Joseph in all the skills needed to become an expert carpenter. In Daniel 1 we read that Daniel, having been taken into captivity, was required to study the language and literature of the Babylonians (his captors). Far from showing resentment or reluctance, Daniel and his companions applied themselves, receiving knowledge and understanding from God (v.17). At the end of their training they were ten times better than all the magicians and enchanters and so were enabled to serve the king and be in positions of influence.

INVESTIGATE:
Read Exodus 35:30–36:7.
Notice the emphasis in this passage on both God-given skills and on training (Exod. 35:34).
- How did you develop the skills you require for your job?
- What part does God-given ability play in your role?
- Have you ever felt reluctant to learn a new skill?
- How proactive have you been in seeking to learn new skills?

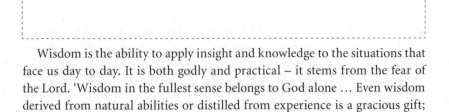

Wisdom is the ability to apply insight and knowledge to the situations that face us day to day. It is both godly and practical – it stems from the fear of the Lord. 'Wisdom in the fullest sense belongs to God alone ... Even wisdom derived from natural abilities or distilled from experience is a gracious gift; because God's creative activity makes such wisdom possible.'[1]

Paul makes it clear in 1 Corinthians 1:20–25 that God's wisdom and the wisdom of the world are often very different. This was brought home to me in a rate negotiation with a key client. I had prayed about it, yet my prayer was of the 'delegation' variety: 'Lord, you know the rate I want to achieve, please get it for me!' Gradually the Lord began to impress upon me that His way was different – I was to go to my client and tell him, up front, that any rate he chose to give me was okay with me!

'Lord, you don't understand – you just don't negotiate that way! Trust me, Lord, I train courses in this stuff – this isn't how you do it!' The Lord answered: 'Trust in the LORD with all your heart and lean not on your own understanding ... Do not be wise in your own eyes ...' (Prov. 3:5,7).

When I told the training manager that he was free to decide the rate and I would accept his decision, his reaction was extraordinary. He had been in a meeting earlier that day with a trainer who had pushed him for a rate that he did not feel he could afford: he had agreed the rate, but decided to give that trainer no further work. As a result of my stance in the negotiation, together with my track record, I was made their 'trainer of choice' and was given my pick of every training project! (The rate agreed was good too!) The decision to trust God's wisdom more than our own abilities, skills and experience is a daily challenge.

INVESTIGATE:
Read Proverbs 2:1–5; James 1:5–7.
- What are the benefits of wisdom?
- In what areas of your work do you need wisdom?
- How can you gain the wisdom you need?

TO PREPARE US FOR PROMOTION

The story of Joseph shows how God prepares us for promotion. In thirteen years Joseph moves from being a shepherd boy to Prime Minister of the whole land of Egypt. Interestingly, Joseph did not instigate a single career move himself and would definitely not have chosen to be either a slave or a prisoner. Yet in each situation he sought to honour both God and his 'employer'.

INVESTIGATE:
Read: Genesis 37:1–4; 39:1–6,20–23; 41:39–46.
- What 'equipped' Joseph to take on the responsibility of being the ruler of the whole land of Egypt?
- The role of prime minister requires both competence and character. What experiences developed Joseph's character?
- Did you choose your current role or, like Joseph, did you end up there through a set of circumstances beyond your control (though not beyond God's!)?
- How is God equipping you?

TO DEVELOP OUR CHARACTER

In God's economy, promotion is never about getting a 'bigger and better' job for the status or pay cheque that it provides. God promotes us so that we can be an even greater channel of blessing to others and in order that godly wisdom and influence is at the heart of the world of business, commerce and the public sector. For God to trust us with increased responsibility He often has to do some serious work on our character. For the arrogant, tale-bearing seventeen-year-old lad to become the discerning and wise ruler of Egypt, Joseph was enrolled for thirteen years in the 'finishing school' of slavery and imprisonment. So effective was this school that, when faced with the brothers who had beaten him up, sold him into slavery and lied to his father, he was able to say:

'"You intended to harm me, but God intended it for good to accomplish what is now being done, the saving of many lives. So then, don't be afraid. I will provide for you and your children." And he reassured them and spoke kindly to them' (Gen. 50:20–21).

INVESTIGATE:
- What work situations or experiences has God used to deepen your character?
- Is there anyone whom you still need to forgive?
- How has your capacity to bless others been expanded throughout your years in the workplace?

A fundamental area of our character God needs to shape/change relates to idolatry – self-idolatry or pride and worship of 'foreign gods'. After forty years, the Israelites enter the promised land – it is a land flowing with milk and honey but is also the land of work. Until this point God supernaturally provided food (manna and quail) and miraculously prevented their clothes and shoes from wearing out. From now on God's provision will be through the crops they plant and harvest, the flocks they shepherd and the vineyards and olive groves they tend. He promises prosperity, provided they are faithful in following His commands, and also warns of two very real dangers. Firstly, pride:

'… when you eat and are satisfied, when you build fine houses and settle down, and when your herds and flocks grow large and your silver and gold increase and all you have is multiplied, then your heart will become proud and you will forget the LORD your God, who brought you … out of the land of slavery … You may say to yourself, "My power and the strength of my hands have produced this wealth for me." But remember the LORD your God, for it is he who gives you the ability to produce wealth …' (Deut. 8:12–14,17–18).

How do we avoid this danger? With thankfulness and obedience:

'When you have eaten and are satisfied, praise the LORD your God for the good land he has given you. Be careful that you do not forget the LORD your God, failing to observe his commands, his laws and his decrees …' (Deut. 8:10–11).

Secondly, 'foreign gods'. The Israelites will now be in close contact with the people of the land:

'Be careful, or you will be enticed to turn away and worship other gods and bow down to them. Then the LORD's anger will burn against you, and he will shut the heavens so that it will not rain and the ground will yield no produce, and you will soon perish from the good land the LORD is giving you' (Deut. 11:16–17).

God wants us to influence our workplace – He desires that godly principles and wisdom permeate the decisions in all boardrooms; that generosity to the poor plays a part in the sourcing of materials; that care for His creation governs manufacturing processes; and that respect for human beings, created in the image of God, underpins all employment practices. Yet to be in the position to influence others also means being in a position to be influenced ourselves. The very opportunity to change the world of work for good carries with it the danger that we will be 'enticed to turn away and worship other gods'.

As a trainer, I visit a variety of workplaces. I'm aware of the vast array of 'foreign gods' worshipped: success, status, targets, security, power, academic achievement, the career ladder, popularity, change, activity – even the pension plan. As with the Canaanites, sacrifices are made to these gods – health, relationships, honesty, integrity, family life and care for others. It's all too easy to be enticed to worship these gods, turning away from the true God.

INVESTIGATE:
- What 'foreign gods' are you aware of in your workplace? Which of these are you sometimes 'enticed' to serve?
- What difficulties or pressures do you face when you seek to live differently from your colleagues and refuse to worship their gods?
- What support from others would help you to resist these pressures?

◎ Pray for each other

- Are there workplace situations or decisions for which you require particular wisdom?
- Think particularly of any work events or people (past or present) that caused you harm or pain. Ask God to heal any wounds and to show you any areas where there is unforgiveness.

THE MISSION STATEMENT

◎ Chill out

Thinking back over the last three studies – what has been the idea, concept or question that has most impacted you?

◎ Think through

Most organisations today have a mission statement. This is a brief statement of the purpose of the company or organisation. The intention of a genuine mission statement is to keep members and users aware of the organisation's purpose, as the examples below illustrate:

- 'To enable people and businesses throughout the world to realise their full potential.' Microsoft
- 'To be our customers' favourite place and way to eat.' McDonalds
- 'To bring inspiration and innovation to every athlete in the world.' Nike
- 'To organise the world's information and make it universally accessible and useful.' Google

The mission statement of the Christian Church was set by its founder over two thousand years ago: '*Therefore go and make disciples of all nations, baptising them in the name of the Father and of the Son and of the Holy Spirit, and teaching them to obey everything I have commanded you*' (Matt. 28:19–20).

Increasingly the workplace is the one place where Christian and non-Christian have to meet, relate and spend significant amounts of time together. The basis for evangelism is known to be relational, and the workplace is where most Christians have the highest number of ongoing relationships. A Christian in work or school spends forty hours a week with, on average, fifty people. Some of these relationships will be more than a casual contact – we have sat next to this person in the same office for years; we've telephoned another regularly for months; we discuss how we spent our weekend every Monday with the same five or six people. We know them and are known. They have seen our attitude to other colleagues, how we react to things going wrong, the standard to which we do our work and even our willingness to get the coffee. In the main, the workplace is where Christians are credible – we do a good job. Also we are transparent – people see the difference Christ makes and whether God really matters to us or not. We talk our co-workers language, understand and share their pressures and concerns, and know what makes people around us tick – we are culturally acclimatised.

What other mission campaign can deliver such marvellous openings and opportunities? None! Also, with Christians in the workplace working increasingly longer hours, the time and energy left for 'evangelism' outside of work is minimal.

INVESTIGATE:
- How many people do you meet/speak to during your average working week?
- With how many of these 'contacts' is there the opportunity to discuss something other than work?
- Share examples of when you have discussed your faith with those at work.
- What difficulties do you face in discussing your faith with colleagues?

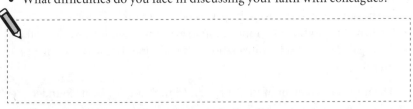

If the workplace now gives us our greatest opportunity for sharing our faith with non-Christians and advancing the mission of the Church, then what stops us witnessing for Christ at work? It is likely that your answer is the same as mine: fear.

This was powerfully brought to my attention at a Diocesan Laity Conference a few years ago. Present were 210 lay Christians exploring the theme, 'Being a Christian at Work'. We split into fourteen groups to discuss, 'What stops you sharing your faith in the workplace?' Every group came back with the same one-word answer: fear. The fear of getting it wrong; not having the answers; having to address the question of suffering; failure; humiliation; lacking credibility; and of what others might think.

INVESTIGATE:
- What things stop you sharing your faith with your work colleagues/customers?
- What fears are you aware of?

So what do we do with this fear? Do we decide that fear justifies us not doing anything? 'Let's just leave it to the confident ones; I'm the wrong personality type …' Do we, as Susan Jeffers' book title says, 'Feel the Fear and Do It Anyway?'[1] Do we rush in and get it all wrong, demonstrating to ourselves and others that our fears were justified? Or is there another way?

INVESTIGATE:
Read Luke 22:54–62; Acts 2:14–24,32–33,36–41.
- How would you describe Peter in his conversations in the Luke 22 passage?
- How would you describe Peter in the Acts 2 passages?
- Which one do you most identify with?
- What do you think had caused the change in Peter?

The change we see in Peter is dramatic – in Luke he is a fearful man who denies his relationship with Jesus, yet in Acts he is a confident preacher, unafraid to call the crowd to repentance. Four key events had happened in between:

- He met with the risen Jesus and was faced with the question: 'Do you love me?' – the motivation for witness.
- He met with other believers to pray – the preparation for witness.
- Jesus told the disciples that 'you will be my witnesses in Jerusalem, and in all Judea and Samaria, and to the ends of the earth' – the strategy for witness.
- He was filled with the Holy Spirit – the power to witness.

MOTIVATION

Three times Jesus questions Peter – 'Do you love me?' (John 21:15–17). I believe that He asks each of us the same question. The only reason we are able to answer 'yes' is because He first loved us:

> We love because he first loved us. If anyone says, 'I love God,' yet hates his brother, he is a liar. For anyone who does not love his brother, whom he has seen, cannot love God, whom he has not seen. And he has given us this command: Whoever loves God must also love his brother.
>
> 1 John 4:19–21

If my love for God is reflected in my love for others, how am I to love my work colleagues? In Week Two we looked at very practical ways of doing this. Beyond this, though, I believe love is shown through having a real concern for their eternal destiny. The Bible speaks of that destiny being either heaven or hell. Without Jesus I fear that my colleagues will miss out on heaven and go to hell. It's a fear that pushes me beyond my comfort zone and motivates me to speak.

Take Barbara. Barbara was the training co-ordinator for a large IT company where I conducted a series of courses. I grew to value her greatly over the months we worked together. Her favourite swear words were 'Jesus Christ', but I was reticent in saying anything for fear of upsetting our friendship. Then, Barbara announced her retirement. In God's wonderful provision, I was conducting training for her company on her final day. I came to the course with a twofold retirement gift: a box of Thornton's chocolates and a book by Michael Green called *Jesus*, which begins: 'For many people Jesus is just a swear word'.[2] (Subtlety was never my strong point!) I explained to Barbara that the trainer in me wanted her to know more about a name she often used. A week or so later, I received this:

> *Hello Beverley,*
> *Just to let you know that the chocolates are nearing the end of the box and the book is interesting. To make me feel less guilty when I want a chocolate, I read the book, so I'm doing well on both counts!*
> *Barbara*

Let your love for Jesus, shown through your love for your colleagues, drive out the fear of speaking to them about Him.

PRAYER

The minute we start to witness, we enter a spiritual battle, and it is a battle we need to take seriously. We have an enemy, the devil, who does not want to see people saved. And he will attack – often acting through others. Read Nehemiah 4 – a great case study on the kind of opposition we may encounter.

INVESTIGATE:
- What tactics did the enemy use to oppose the Israelites rebuilding the wall?
- How did the Israelites counter these attacks?

My own experience is that after praying and asking others to pray, opportunities to speak about my faith come. I'd like to say that I always take those opportunities, but that's not the case. Yet God is faithful, even when I am not, and, as I repent of my silence, He gives new opportunities to speak.

Praying with others both encourages us and reminds us that we are part of the body of Christ – even when we are feeling isolated in our workplace. You may want to form prayer partnerships or triplets with others from your church – perhaps linking by email as well as meeting together. Meeting with other Christians at work for prayer is also vital if we are to see significant change in our organisational or team culture – I know of some groups in the City of London who meet for prayer (and strong coffee!) at 7.30am once a week.

STRATEGY

Whilst it is natural and right to bring our own workplace requests to God in prayer, it is also important to listen and hear from Him how we should pray for the organisation. In this listening we may find that He asks us to repent on behalf of the organisation for any wrong practices we are aware of (see Nehemiah's prayer in Nehemiah 1:5–11); He may bring to mind certain individuals He wants us to pray for; He may highlight attitudes, hurts and blockages that are a barrier to His Spirit moving in power.[3]

As we pray in this way, God will reveal His strategy and show us who/where our Jerusalem, Judea and Samaria are. One Christian told me how God showed him who to intercede for and what barriers (pride, bitterness etc) prevented this person from turning to Christ. He then prayed specifically into these areas. Intercession like this may involve prayer with fasting. As I prayed for one large public organisation for whom I was running a board development programme, God indicated a spiritual barrier preventing the board engaging with positive change. A group of us prayed with fasting. We saw that barrier pulled down and radical change take place in the way the board operated.

INVESTIGATE:
- Who can you/do you pray with concerning workplace issues?
- What might a prayer strategy look like for your place of work/team?

POWER

What does God expect from you at work? The answer is 'nothing'! John makes this quite clear: '... Apart from me you can do nothing' (John 15:5). Even Jesus could do nothing through His own efforts: 'Rather, it is the Father, living in me, who is doing his work' (John 14:10).

It is God's breath, His Spirit, in us that does the work of reproducing the character of Jesus in us, of changing us into His likeness and of fulfilling His purposes and plans for our workplace. This doesn't mean that we have no role in this transformation or that we are passive. We can either co-operate with God's Spirit or grieve Him. We can either respond to Him or quench Him. We grieve the Holy Spirit when we fail to allow Him to do that for which He was given to us. He can also be quenched. Every time the Spirit whispers 'This is the way, walk ye in it' we are faced with a choice – to walk God's way or to go our own way. If we have consistently ignored the Spirit's promptings we will become deaf to His voice – we will have quenched His activity in our lives.

Yet the good news is: 'If a man remains in me and I in him, he will bear much fruit; apart from me you can do nothing' (John 15:5). You see, nothing is impossible for God (see Luke 1:37)!

If we allow Him to work through us then we will see miracles. A phrase that has both challenged and encouraged me is: 'If you seek God's presence in the private place you will know His presence in the public place.' I don't know about you, but I want to know God's presence every day of my working life!

INVESTIGATE:
- Share examples of when you have known God's presence in your workplace.

Pray for each other

- That we might each have the courage to speak to our colleagues about our faith
- That God would give us wisdom as to what to say and when to say it
- That God would reveal His strategy for our workplaces
- That we would increasingly be aware of His presence

Notes

Introduction:

1. Mark Greene, 'The Great Divide: Overcoming the SSD Syndrome', *The Patmos Papers* (Belfast: Centre for Contemporary Christianity in Ireland, 2002).

Week One:

1. John Stott, *Issues Facing Christians Today* (London: Marshall Morgan & Scott, 1984).
2. John Atherton, 'Work', *A Dictionary of Pastoral Care,* ed. Alistair V. Campbell (London: SPCK, 1987) pp. 296–7.
3. Graham Dow, *A Christian Understanding of Daily Work* (Cambridge: Grove Books Ltd, 1994) p.8.
4. Ibid., p.7.
5. Mark Greene, *Thank God it's Monday* (Bletchley: Scripture Union, 3rd edn, 2001) p.122.

Week Two:

1. Eugene Peterson, *A Long Obedience in the Same Direction* (Illinois: IVP, 2000).
2. Adapted from *Weekly Words,* 9 July 2004, distributed by influence@workplaceinfluence.org
3. Os Guinness, *The Call* (Nashville: Word Publishing, 1998) p.28.

Week Three:

1. 'Wisdom', *New Bible Dictionary* (Leicester: IVP, 1982) p.1256.

Week Four:

1. Susan Jeffers, *Feel the Fear and Do It Anyway* (New York: Ballantine Books, 1988).
2. Michael Green, *Jesus* (Guildford: Eagle, 1999).
3. An excellent book on prayer strategy is: Cindy Jacobs, *Possessing the Gates of the Enemy* (London: Marshall Pickering, 1993).